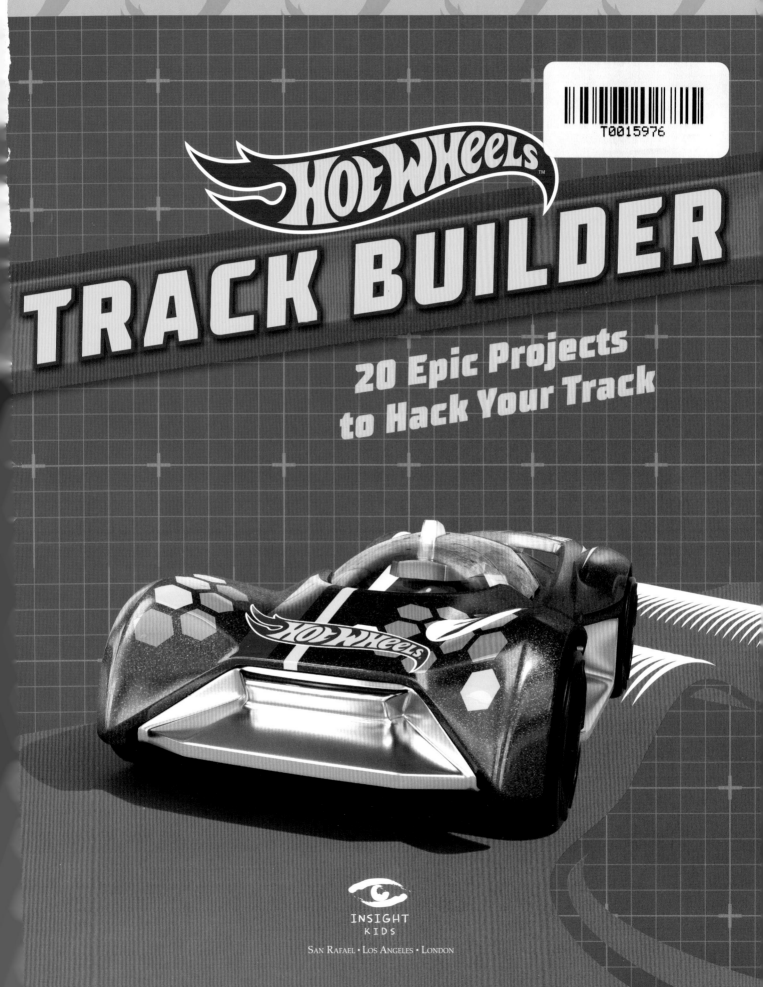

HOT WHEELS™
TRACK BUILDER

20 Epic Projects to Hack Your Track

INSIGHT
KIDS

SAN RAFAEL · LOS ANGELES · LONDON

DROP 'N' LAUNCH

3-2-1 blastoff! Sure, you can use your finger to launch your cars, but why not try something cooler?

YOU'LL NEED

- Something to drop
- Hot Wheels™ paddle launcher
- Hot Wheels™ track riser
- Hot Wheels™ straight track
- Hot Wheels™ car

1

Connect the track to the launcher.

Make sure you get a grown-up's permission and help before doing this awesome hack!

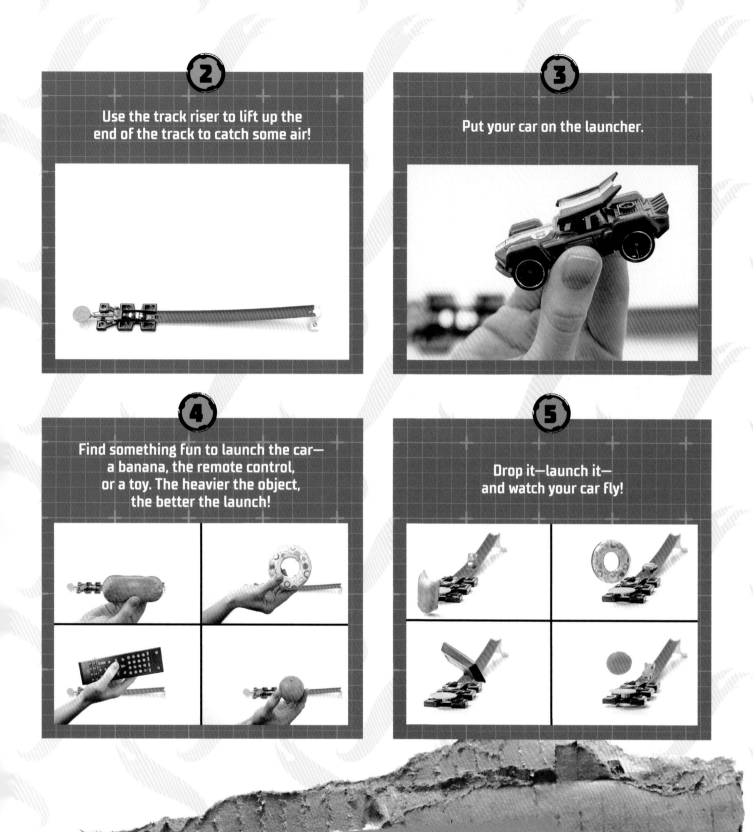

② Use the track riser to lift up the end of the track to catch some air!

③ Put your car on the launcher.

④ Find something fun to launch the car—a banana, the remote control, or a toy. The heavier the object, the better the launch!

⑤ Drop it—launch it—and watch your car fly!

EPIC STEM FACT

You launched the car! In basic terms, you moved it. In science, this means you've changed the car's position compared to something that isn't moving.

TOUGH TRACKS

YOU'LL NEED

- 1 large cardboard box
- 1 sheet of black poster board
- 6 books
- Scissors
- String
- Patterned packing tape
- Hot Wheels™ paddle launcher
- Hot Wheels™ straight track
- Hot Wheels™ cars

Get ready for some epic car crashes when you build this half-pipe tough track!

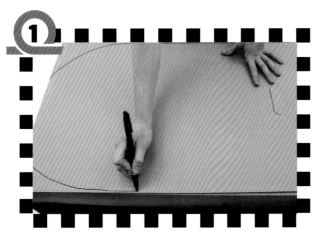

1

Draw a large U shape on the two longest sides of your cardboard box. Go as close to the edges as you can. Then cut out the two U's. Your box should look like a half-pipe.

2

Slide the black poster board inside of the box to line your half-pipe. Use cool-patterned packing tape to attach the poster board to the edges of the box.

Make sure you get a grown-up's permission and help before doing this awesome hack!

3

Make two stacks of books. Cut two long pieces of string. Tie one end of a string around one stack of books. Then poke a hole at the top of one half-pipe wall and tie off the other end of the string. Repeat these steps for the second set of string and books for the other half-pipe wall. This will keep the half-pipe stable.

4

Tape a piece of track on one side of the half-pipe for launching your cars from the top.

5

Attach the paddle launcher to a piece of track and aim it at the middle of your half-pipe.

6

Challenge a friend! Have them launch a car from the top of the half-pipe while you launch a car from the paddle launcher. Then wait for the crash!

EPIC STEM FACT

Two cars striking into each other = a collision. The cars exert a force on each other when they collide, making them bounce off each other and swerve off course.

WATER WHEELS

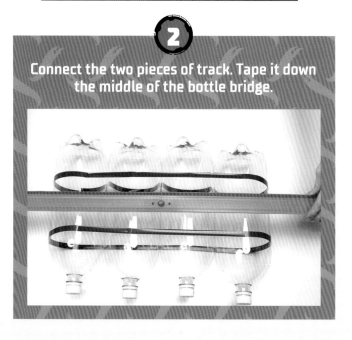

Boats aren't the only vehicles that can make a splash!

YOU'LL NEED

5 clean, empty 1-liter bottles
Electrical tape
1 large plastic container filled 3/4 full with water
2 long pieces of Hot Wheels™ track
Hot Wheels™ car

1

Lay four of the bottles side-by-side, and tape them together with two rows of tape.

2

Connect the two pieces of track. Tape it down the middle of the bottle bridge.

Make sure you get a grown-up's permission and help before doing this awesome hack!

3

Set the bottles on top of the water in the plastic container so that the ends of the track overlap the edges of the container, forming a bridge. Then your cars can race safely over the water.

4

A bridge is fun, but a ramp is better! Take everything out of the water and dry it off. Remove the track, and then stack the last bottle on top of the row of bottles with tape.

5

Attach the end of the track to the new bottle with tape, forming a ramp. Then set the bottles back in the water at the edge of the container.

6

Send your car flying off the ramp and into the water for a spectacular splash!

EPIC STEM FACT

Water sprays when the falling car smashes against it. The splash is water being forced to move when a falling object hits it.

RAPID-FIRE LAUNCHER

4-3-2-1! Launch four cars at once!

YOU'LL NEED

- 2 same-size cardboard boxes taped closed
- Black poster board
- 2 empty cardboard wrapping paper tubes
- Straws
- 10 clean craft sticks
- Two 12-inch rulers
- Scissors
- Patterned packing tape
- Electrical tape
- Hot Wheels™ track
- Hot Wheels™ cars
- Hot Wheels™ loop track

1

Join the two cardboard boxes together using your patterned tape.

2

Cut the boxes to create a large triangle that juts up at the top.

3

Stand up your triangle box, and tape the black poster board inside of the open portion to create a road. Tape straws to the edges of the road. This is the ramp.

Make sure you get a grown-up's permission and help before doing this awesome hack!

4

Cover the cardboard tubes in patterned tape. Cut four slits at equal intervals in each tube. Slide the craft sticks into the slits to join the tubes together. Tape the craft sticks in place. This is your lever. Tape the remaining craft sticks end-to-end down the middle of the black poster board road on your ramp.

5

Now it's time to attach the ramp and lever together. Use scissors to poke two holes at the very top of the ramp, one on each side. Poke one hole on each side of one end of the lever. Hold the lever at the top of the ramp and line up the holes. Poke a straw through the holes on each side of the ramp and lever to attach the lever. Your lever should lift up and down with ease.

6

Tape a piece of track at the bottom of the ramp. It should be attached perpendicular to the ramp. Then tape a ruler to the outside edge of the track—this rail will keep your cars from flying off the track.

7

Create a maze of track that includes a loop-de-loop, and attach it to the track coming off the ramp. Now you're ready to race! With the lever closed, place four cars on the four craft-stick rungs on the lever.

8

Lift up the lever and drop and drive!

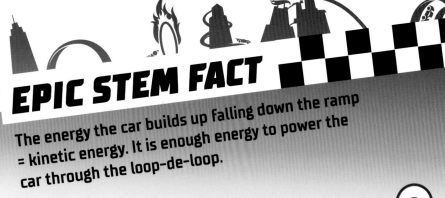

EPIC STEM FACT

The energy the car builds up falling down the ramp = kinetic energy. It is enough energy to power the car through the loop-de-loop.

BIG BALLOON RACERS

Ready for a party? Race your cars inside of a balloon!

YOU'LL NEED

- Balloons—light colors work best
- 1 short cardboard tube (cut an empty toilet paper tube in half)
- Electrical tape
- Hot Wheels™ cars
- Hot Wheels™ track
- 2 Hot Wheels™ adjustable clamps

1

Stretch the opening of the balloon around one end of the short tube, creating a tunnel into the balloon. Slide your car inside.

Make sure you get a grown-up's permission and help before doing this awesome hack!

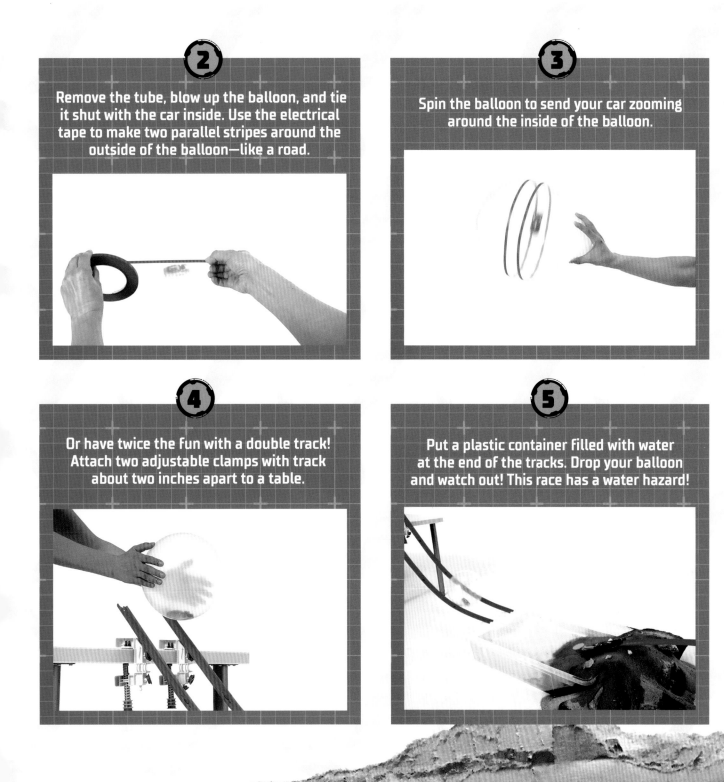

②

Remove the tube, blow up the balloon, and tie it shut with the car inside. Use the electrical tape to make two parallel stripes around the outside of the balloon—like a road.

③

Spin the balloon to send your car zooming around the inside of the balloon.

④

Or have twice the fun with a double track! Attach two adjustable clamps with track about two inches apart to a table.

⑤

Put a plastic container filled with water at the end of the tracks. Drop your balloon and watch out! This race has a water hazard!

EPIC STEM FACT

What keeps the car moving in a circular path around the curve of the inside of the balloon? Centripetal force! Spinning a ball on a string or twirling lassos are all examples of centripetal force.

HOT WHEELS™ MUSICAL

Rock out with your favorite Hot Wheels™ racers!

YOU'LL NEED

1 musical instrument—a drum, xylophone, or tambourine
1 thick book
Hot Wheels™ tall track riser with base
Hot Wheels™ track
Hot Wheels™ cars

1 Set your track riser with base on a book. If it feels wobbly, tape it to the book for added stability.

2 Attach a long piece of track to the riser.

Make sure you get a grown-up's permission and help before doing this awesome hack!

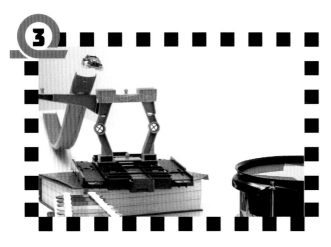

3 Place an instrument about 6 inches away from the ramp. Then race your car up the ramp and send it soaring to hit those high notes!

Adjust the track, ramp, or instrument to make that perfect landing.

5 Try it with different instruments and pick your favorite sound!

EPIC STEM FACT

The car makes the instrument vibrate upon impact. Sounds are created from these vibrations when the vibrating waves of air reach your ear.

SUPERDOMINOS

Set off a charged-up chain reaction with these giant dominos!

YOU'LL NEED

- 3 empty rectangular cardboard boxes of varying sizes (e.g., crackers, mac and cheese, cereal)
- White wrapping paper
- Markers
- Scissors
- Glue
- Construction paper
- 1 set of dominos
- Hot Wheels™ paddle launcher
- Hot Wheels™ 2-lane launcher connected to track
- Hot Wheels™ cars

1

Wrap the three boxes in white paper and decorate them to look like dominos. Draw the spots and lines with markers, or cut the shapes out of construction paper and glue them on. These are your superdominos.

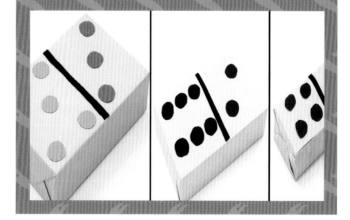

Make sure you get a grown-up's permission and help before doing this awesome hack!

2

Arrange the regular dominos in a triangular formation.

3

Set the paddle launcher in front of the domino triangle. Then place the superdominos in size order in front of the launcher. The last superdomino should hit the paddle launcher when it falls. Place the 2-lane launcher in front of the superdominos. (You may need to prop it up on a book.)

4

Place two cars in the 2-lane launcher and one car in the paddle launcher. First release the 2-lane launcher to send both cars racing down the track. Crash! They hit the first superdomino!

5

The last superdomino will fall, hit the paddle launcher, and launch the car into the regular dominos for an epic knockdown!

EPIC STEM FACT

A chain reaction is a sequence of events where one thing triggers the next thing, which triggers the next, and on and on.

EXTREME EXPERT

Ready, Set, Race! Send 12 cars flying down your own custom racetrack. May the best car win!

YOU'LL NEED

- 1 large, rectangular cardboard box taped closed
- Scissors
- 2 empty cardboard wrapping paper tubes
- Three 12-inch rulers
- 1 yardstick
- Patterned packing tape
- Hot Wheels™ tracks
- 12 Hot Wheels™ cars

1
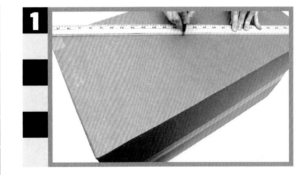

Turn the cardboard box on its longest side. Use the yardstick to draw a diagonal line between opposite corners. Cut along that line. This will make a large ramp.

2

Customize and make it cool! Use patterned packing tape to decorate the ramp and cardboard tubes.

Make sure you get a grown-up's permission and help before doing this awesome hack!

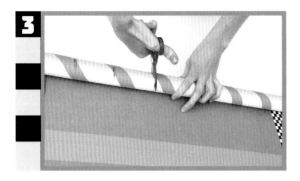

3 Attach the cardboard tubes on each side of the ramp with tape. Cut three slits at the top of each tube. The slits should be evenly spaced and line up with the slits in the other tube.

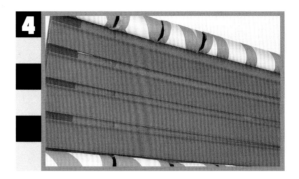

4 Tape four pieces of same-length track between the two tubes on your ramp. Align the top of the tracks to the top of the ramp.

5 Slide the rulers into the slits on each tube to create three rows. Place cars on each track in all three rows.

6 Lift the rulers one at a time to release 4 cars. Do it fast enough and you'll have all 12 cars racing at once!

EPIC STEM FACT

Speed! It's how we measure how fast something moves from point a to point b. The faster the car gets to its destination, the more speed it has. Which car was the speediest?

MAGIC BOX

Mad science hack! Amaze your friends when this cool creation totally transforms your car!

YOU'LL NEED

- 1 empty shoebox
- 2 empty cardboard toilet paper tubes
- Construction paper
- Scissors
- Paint
- Black and yellow pipe cleaners
- Tape
- Hot Wheels™ track
- 2 Hot Wheels™ cars
- Hot Wheels™ track riser

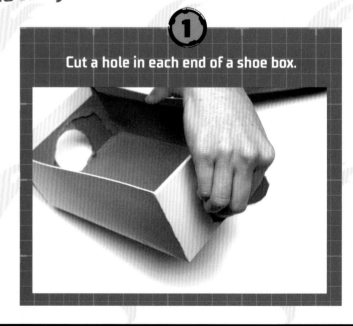

1

Cut a hole in each end of a shoe box.

Make sure you get a grown-up's permission and help before doing this awesome hack!

2

Slide a piece of track through the holes. Cut a square of construction paper as wide and tall as the shoebox, and fold it at the bottom. Then tape the paper on top of the track in the middle of the shoebox to separate the box into two sections.

3

Place one car on the right side of the box on the track, with its back against the paper. The other car will speed into the box, hit the paper, and push the first car out the other end of the box. The car will seem magically changed!

4

Put the lid on the box. Paint two cardboard tubes and wrap them in curled black pipe cleaners. Attach black and yellow pipe cleaners to the tubes to look like an electrical current. Tape the tubes to the top of your box and add some paper lightning bolts.

5

Connect a track riser to the track that enters the first half of the box. Add additional track to the track that exits the other half of the box. Now you're ready to race!

6

Launch your car and amaze your friends!

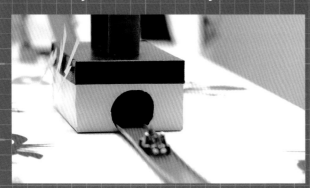

EPIC STEM FACT

The magic is caused by force! The first car transfers its force energy to the second car, sending it racing away.

SKEE CAR

Take car jumps to the extreme with a Hot Wheels™ Skee Board!

YOU'LL NEED

1 clean, empty pizza box
Scissors
Markers
Masking tape
Hot Wheels™ straight track
Hot Wheels™ booster
Hot Wheels™ car

1

Draw a triangle, a circle, and a square in a vertical line down the middle of the bottom part of a pizza box. Cut out each shape to become holes in the pizza box.

2

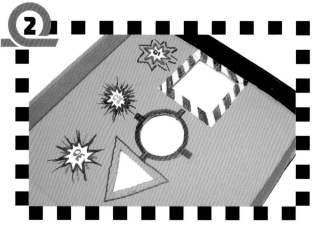

Write 10 next to the square-shaped hole, 20 next to the circle-shaped hole, and 30 next to the triangle-shaped hole. Then decorate the pizza box.

Make sure you get a grown-up's permission and help before doing this awesome hack!

3

Bend back the lid of the pizza box and tape it on the sides so that the box sits up on its own.

4

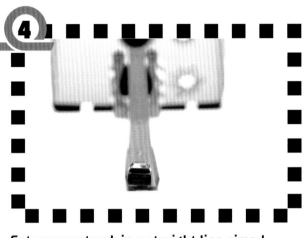

Set up your track in a straight line aimed at the pizza box with a riser at the end to lift up the track.

5

Race your car down the track, jump through the holes, and gain some points—10 points through the square, 20 points through the circle, and 30 points through the triangle!

6

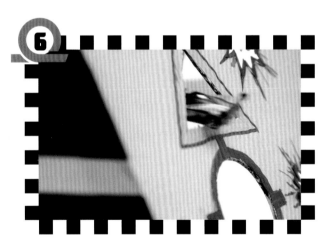

Adjust the position of your track and ramp height until your cars zoom through the holes.

EPIC STEM FACT

The slope of the ramp affects how steep it is. Changing the slope will change the car's path of motion, letting you score big points!

MONSTER TRUCK TIRE TRACKS

Who needs brushes? Grab your monster trucks and let the creativity roll!

YOU'LL NEED

1 giant piece of white poster board
Straws
6 paper bowls
1 paper plate
Scissors
Patterned packing tape
4 different colors of paint
2 pieces of Hot Wheels™ track
Hot Wheels™ monster truck

1

It's gonna get messy! Ask a grown-up for the best spot to set up. Place your poster board on the floor, and tape the straws on the edges to see where the poster board ends.

2

Tape five paper bowls upside-down on the poster board. Make sure two bowls have their edges touching. Prop the last bowl right-side up against those two. Cut the center out of the paper plate, and tape the paper ring over the propped-up bowl.

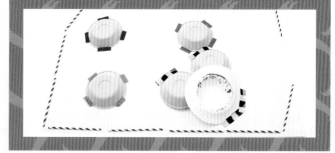

Make sure you get a grown-up's permission and help before doing this awesome hack!

Pour some paint on the top of each upside-down bowl. Next fill the propped-up bowl about 1/3 of the way full with the last paint color.

Place the track at the entrance and drive your monster truck into your very own art arena!

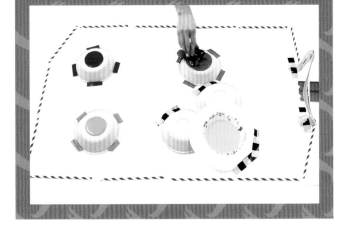

Splash through the paint pits! Drive all over the poster board, and the wheels will leave awesome art tire tracks.

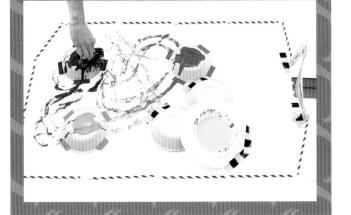

For the finale, have your truck splash down in the big pool of paint in the propped-up bowl!

EPIC STEM FACT

Red, yellow, and blue are primary colors. When you mix these colors together, they make other colors. Mix the red paint with the blue paint and the yellow paint with the blue paint. What colors were you able to make?

CUP WHEEL DISPENSER

Get your wheels spinning with this rotating Hot Wheels™ dispenser.

YOU'LL NEED

Two 1-liter bottles of soda or water

2 thick paper plates

Markers

Construction paper

1 wooden dowel

3 short plastic cups

Tape

Scissors

Metal brads (2 per cup)

Hot Wheels™ track

Hot Wheels™ cars

1 Trace the bottom of a cup on colored construction paper, then cut and tape the paper circles to the bottom of each cup. Cut an opening on one side of each plastic cup.

2 Poke a hole the same width as your wooden dowel in the center of two paper plates. Decorate both paper plates with swirls.

Make sure you get a grown-up's permission and help before doing this awesome hack!

3

Attach the paper plates to the cups. Punch a metal brad through the edge of one paper plate. Then punch the same brad through the side of one of the plastic cups. Do this again with the second paper plate on the other side of the cup.

4

Repeat the same process with the other two cups to finish your cup wheel. Make sure all of the cups face the same direction with the openings on the outside of the wheel.

5

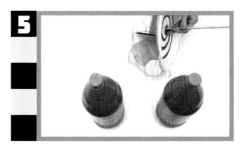

Run the wooden dowel through the middle of both paper plates.

6

Tape each end of the dowel to the top of each soda bottle.

7

Hold a piece of track above the wheel and race your car off of it. The car will land in a cup, spinning the wheel!

EPIC STEM FACT

The kinetic energy built up from the moving car is transferred to the wheel when the car falls in, creating mechanical energy, and making the wheel spin. The more kinetic energy the car has, the more mechanical energy will be created and the faster the wheel will spin.

SCOOP JUMP

YOU'LL NEED

- 1 large, rectangular cardboard box taped closed
- Masking tape
- Patterned packing tape
- Markers
- Scissors
- Construction paper
- Poster board
- Hot Wheels™ track
- Hot Wheels™ track connector
- Hot Wheels™ car

Get massive air on this awesome scoop jump!

1

Draw a scoop shape on your box and cut it out, leaving a small half-pipe.

Make sure you get a grown-up's permission and help before doing this awesome hack!

2

Flip over your scoop jump. Then cut out a piece of poster board the same width as the scoop jump, and tape it to the edges of the jump.

3

Decorate the jump using patterned tape, construction paper, and markers.

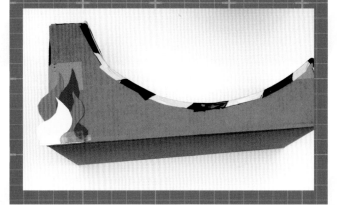

4

Add the track connector to the track. Cut a small slit in the middle at the high end of the jump. Slide the track connecter into the slit so the track sticks up at the top of the jump.

5

Drop your car onto the track and watch it fly!

EPIC STEM FACT

Gravity! It's what makes the car accelerate downward. Acceleration means the car picks up speed as it falls. The car's speed at the bottom of the ramp is greater than at the top of the ramp.

TRACK TILTERS

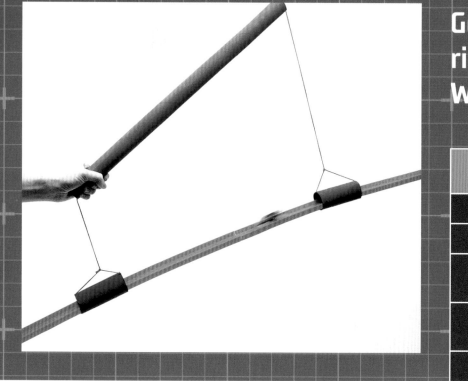

Get ready for a wild ride on this Hot Wheels™ tilting track!

YOU'LL NEED
String
Scissors
1 empty cardboard wrapping paper tube
2 empty cardboard toilet paper tubes
Paint
Hot Wheels™ track
Hot Wheels™ car

1

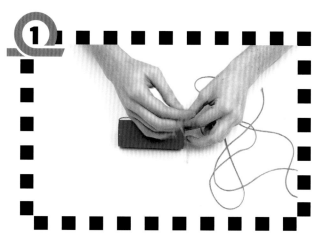

Paint and decorate your cardboard tubes. Cut one superlong piece of string. Thread one end of the string through the first toilet paper tube and tie it on top.

2

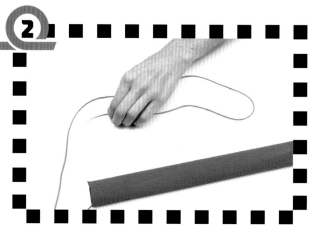

Then thread the other end of the string all the way through the long wrapping paper tube.

Make sure you get a grown-up's permission and help before doing this awesome hack!

3

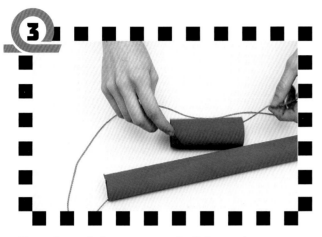

Now thread the same end of the string through the other toilet paper tube and tie it on top.

4

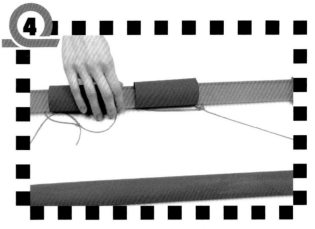

Connect several pieces of track together. Then slide the track into both of the toilet paper tubes to finish your tilter.

5

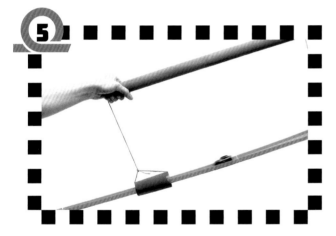

Hold the tilter by the wrapping paper tube. Adjust the two toilet paper tubes so that you can hold the tilter level.

6

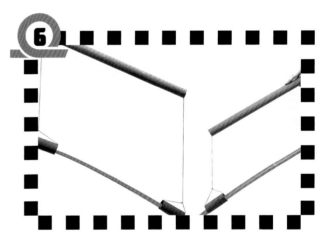

Add a car to the track and send it zooming back and forth with even the smallest movement of your hand.

EPIC STEM FACT

Changing the angle = changing the car's path of motion. The car will always travel down the ramp.

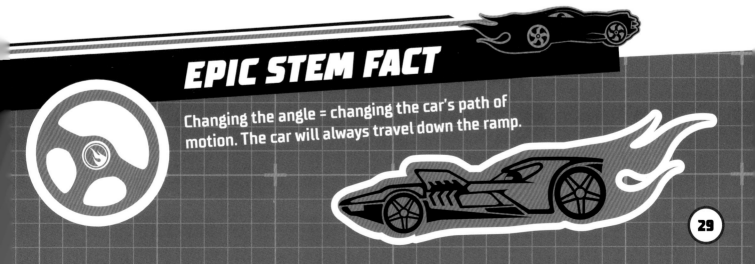

HOT WHEELS™ SNAKE

Slither at superspeeds with this epic chain of Hot Wheels™ cars.

YOU'LL NEED

String
Tape
2 clothespins
Hot Wheels™ cars
Hot Wheels™ tracks

1

Turn your cars over and place them in a line about an inch apart.

2

Cut a long piece of string and tape it to the bottom of the cars.

Make sure you get a grown-up's permission and help before doing this awesome hack!

3

Flip over the cars and place them on the track.

4

Pull the front car along the track and the rest will follow!

5

Make a figure-8 racetrack. Use the clothespins to hold the top track above the bottom track.

6

Make a superlong Hot Wheels™ snake and watch it slide along the entire track!

EPIC STEM FACT

Pulling on the chained cars means you are applying a force. A bigger pull means a greater force, which makes the chain of cars speed up.

TUBE JUMP

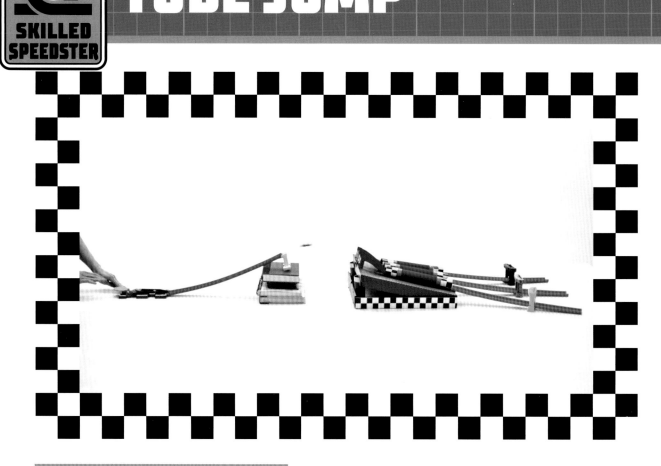

YOU'LL NEED

- 1 clean, empty pizza box
- A stack of books
- Masking tape
- 3 empty cardboard paper towel tubes
- 2 empty cardboard toilet paper tubes
- Hot Wheels™ paddle launcher
- 3 Hot Wheels™ gates
- 3 Hot Wheels™ red ramps
- Hot Wheels™ short white ramp
- Hot Wheels™ tracks
- Hot Wheels™ cars

3 tubes. 3 ramps.
3 legendary landings!

1

Decorate your cardboard tubes and pizza box. Insert a red ramp into each paper towel tube.

Make sure you get a grown-up's permission and help before doing this awesome hack!

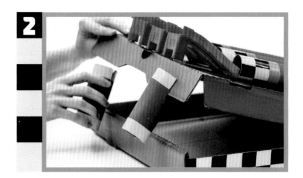

2

Line up the ramp tubes on top of the pizza box lid, and attach them with tape. Cut two slits into each end of the toilet paper tubes, and use them to hold the pizza box partially open.

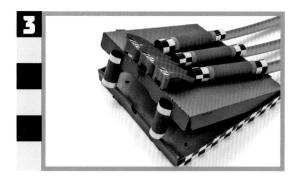

3

Insert track into the end of each tube. Add a gate on each piece of track.

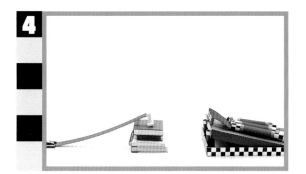

4

Across from the pizza box opening, attach the paddle launcher to a long piece of track that ends in a short ramp on a stack of books.

5

Launch your cars and try to get them to each land on a different ramp to raise all three gates!

EPIC STEM FACT

With enough kinetic energy, the car will accelerate down the track, launch off the ramp, and sail across the gap. If you don't supply the car with enough energy, the car will stall.

MORE WATER WHEELS

Race to a splashdown with this cool floating Hot Wheels™ track!

YOU'LL NEED

- 1 pool noodle
- Electrical tape
- Scissors
- 1 plastic container filled 3/4 full of water
- 1 cardboard box
- Hot Wheels™ tracks
- Hot Wheels™ cars

1 Cut the pool noodle in half, lengthwise.

Make sure you get a grown-up's permission and help before doing this awesome hack!

2

Set the two pieces of pool noodle next to each other and tape them together.

3

Tape track along the length of each pool noodle half.

4

Prop up one end of the floating racetrack on the cardboard box, and set the other end in the container of water.

5

Race two cars to see which can splash down first!

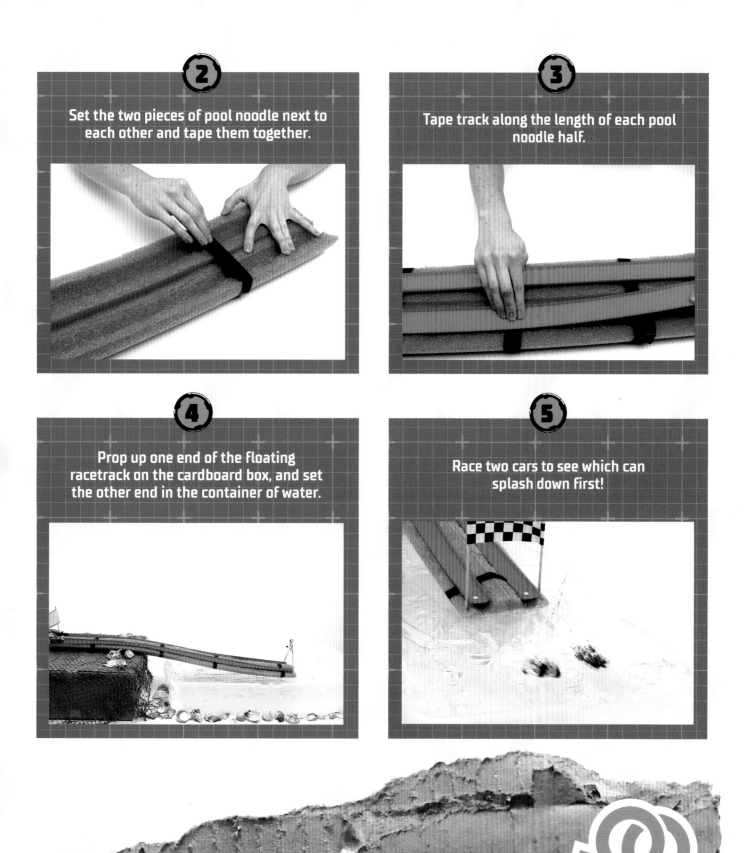

EPIC STEM FACT

Do the cars sink or float when they strike the water? If the downward force of gravity is greater than the upward force of the water, the car will sink.

MOVIE BACKDROP

Make your own moving backdrop and film your favorite Hot Wheels™ racers!

YOU'LL NEED

- 2 paper towel holders
- 2 empty, cardboard paper towel tubes
- White printer paper
- Clear tape
- Colored pencils or crayons
- 1 smartphone or digital camera that can take video
- Hot Wheels™ track piece
- Hot Wheels™ car

1

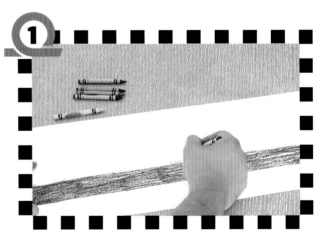

Tape two pieces of white paper together. Flip over the paper and draw a long road scene on it. Then tape the ends of the paper together to form a large paper loop.

Make sure you get a grown-up's permission and help before doing this awesome hack!

2

Place the paper towel holders close together, and slide the empty cardboard tubes onto the holders. Then slide the looped scene down over the tubes.

3

Place the track in front of the scene and put your car on the track.

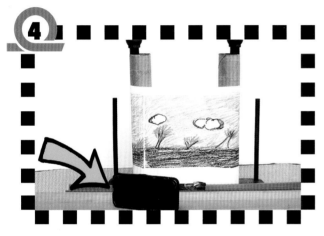 

4

Set up your camera pointing at the scene. Make sure only the backdrop, track, and car are seen in your shot.

5

Hit Record. Hold the track still while turning the cardboard tube slowly so that the scene moves on a loop.

6

Once you've turned the loop a few times, use editing software to finish your movie and show it to your friends!

EPIC STEM FACT

Even if the car itself isn't moving, the shifting frames of the movie backdrop make your brain think the car is moving.

PYRAMID JUMPERS

ROOKIE RACER

Race your cars through your very own pyramids with this totally tubular hack!

YOU'LL NEED

42 empty cardboard toilet paper tubes (21 tubes per pyramid)
Paint
1 paintbrush
Masking tape
Markers
Hot Wheels™ track
Hot Wheels™ car

1

Paint the tubes and then let them dry.

2

Tape the tubes together, stacking to form a pyramid. Place six tubes on the bottom row, five on the next row, then four, three, two, until one on top. Make two pyramids.

Make sure you get a grown-up's permission and help before doing this awesome hack!

3

Set the pyramids about one foot apart on the ground. Tape each pyramid to the floor using masking tape.

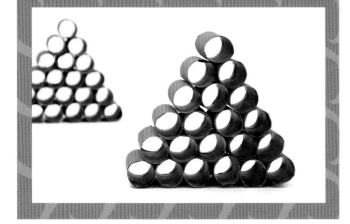

4

Make the track as long as you like. Then thread the track through one tube in each pyramid. Tape the track to the edge of the tube for extra stability.

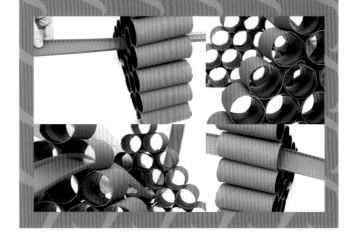

5

Now you're ready to race! Hold one end of the track up high and drop your car onto the track!

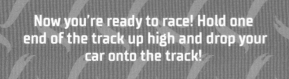

6

Watch your car zoom through tricky tunnels and tubes.

EPIC STEM FACT

Potential energy! It's what the car at the top of the track has. It's not going anywhere but has the potential to go somewhere. When the car rolls down the track, the potential energy becomes kinetic energy giving the car motion.

SKILLED SPEEDSTER

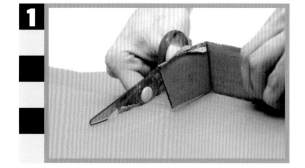

Go bonkers for Hot Wheels™ bumper cars!

YOU'LL NEED

- 1 clean, empty pizza box
- Scissors
- Masking tape
- White paper
- Markers
- Patterned packing tape
- 3 friends—this one's a team hack!
- 4 balloons
- Hot Wheels™ cars

1 Cut the lid off of the pizza box. Then cut four rectangular strips of cardboard out of the lid. Each strip should be about one inch wide and four inches long.

2 Tape a cardboard strip diagonally across each corner of the pizza box.

Make sure you get a grown-up's permission and help before doing this awesome hack!

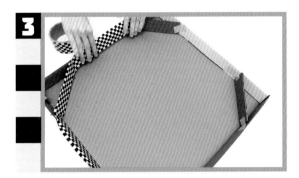

3

Decorate the box with patterned tape and your own awesome art style.

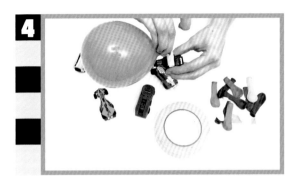

4

Put a small loop of tape on the top of four cars. Then blow up four balloons, but don't tie them closed; hold them closed with your fingers. Then stick one balloon on the tape loop on top of each car. Hold the car and the balloon together to keep the air in.

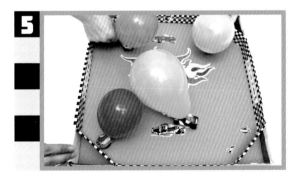

5

Release the cars! The air rushing out of the balloons propels the cars in a crazy, crashing race around the box.

6

The last car racing is the winner!

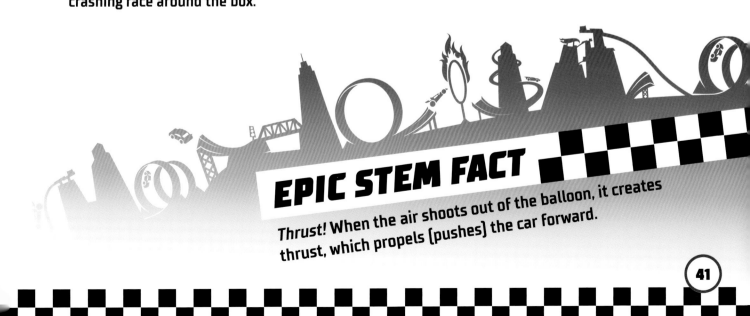

EPIC STEM FACT

Thrust! When the air shoots out of the balloon, it creates thrust, which propels (pushes) the car forward.

CHECK OUT THESE AMAZING STEM FACTS!

MOTION COMMOTION

Now that you've zipped, zoomed, whizzed, and whooshed your Hot Wheels cars up, down, over, and around these courses, let's take a pit stop and think about what's going on.

What do all of these awesome Hot Wheels hacks have in common? Motion! You made the car move in super cool ways! Movement and motion are always happening around you, even if you don't realize it. A breeze is the movement of air. Waves crashing against the shore is the movement of water. The sound of a car horn is the movement of vibrations that reach your ear. The Earth is in constant motion around the sun. Motion is happening everywhere!

MORE THAN JUST AN APPLE

There's a famous story about the scientist Isaac Newton. One day, while Newton was sitting under an apple tree, he was hit in the head by a falling apple. As legend has it, the apple falling from the tree made Newton "discover" the force of gravity. While the story is super cool, nobody really knows if it's true. What is true is that Newton did make some very important discoveries about motion. These discoveries are called Newton's three laws of motion.

HOW MOTION WORKS

Think about all the directions your cars moved in the hacks of this book. Motion can be upward, downward, right, left, and even round and round.

But the motion of the cars didn't happen on its own. You had to do something to the car to get it moving. You may have pushed the car, pulled the car, or launched the car, but in all cases, you did *something* to get the car going. What you did was supply the car with energy by applying a **force**.

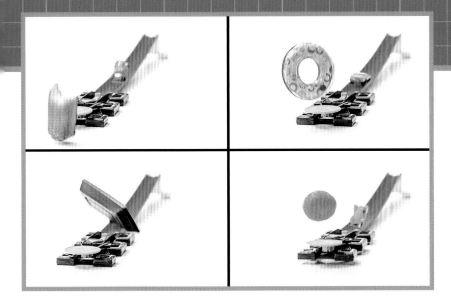

NEWTON'S FIRST LAW

An object at rest will stay at rest until a force acts on it.

Think about it this way . . . if a toy car is resting on the table, it's not going to move anywhere unless someone comes along and picks it up, rolls it, or pushes it.

NEWTON'S SECOND LAW

Two things affect an object's motion: how big the object is and how much force is used.

Imagine you have two identical toy cars. If you push them both with different amounts of force, the car you push with more force will travel farther.

Now, imagine you have two different toy cars: a big one and a small one. If you push the big car with the same amount of force as the small car, the small car will travel farther because it has less mass.

NEWTON'S THIRD LAW

For every action there is an equal and opposite reaction.

When you push a toy car with your hand, you are exerting a force on it. You may not feel it, but the car actually exerts an equal force back against your hand.

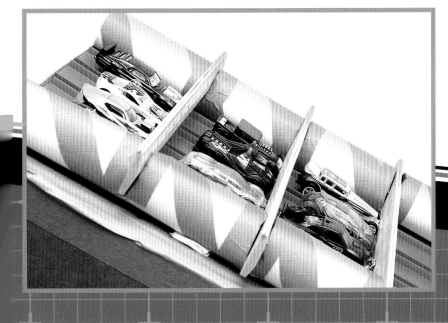

Forces are what gives an object motion. When you push or pull on an object, you're exerting a force on that object. The force you apply provides energy to the car to set it in motion. But forces also keep the car moving, stop it from moving, and change the car's direction. Without forces, motion isn't possible.

Gravity is a special kind of force that pulls things downward. When you drop something, it falls down. When you jump up, you come down. How many of the hacks in this book relied on gravity to make the car go?

Forces give an object the energy it needs to move. When an object is getting ready to move, it is bursting with **potential energy**. This potential energy is stored within the object just before it is set in motion. Once the object begins to move, the potential energy is converted into **kinetic energy**. Think of kinetic energy as the energy of motion. The more kinetic energy an object has, the faster or farther it can travel.

GRAVITY FUN FACT

Gravity affects the weight of an object. The moon's gravity is about 1/6 the Earth's gravity, so objects on the moon will weigh less than on Earth. So if you weigh 100 pounds on Earth, you would weigh just under 17 pounds on the moon!

ALL ABOUT SPEED

When a car is in motion, it has <u>speed</u>. Speed is a measure of how fast the car is moving. When you say a car is traveling at a speed of 30 miles per hour, what you're saying is that it will take the car 1 hour to drive 30 miles. Fast cars travel at higher speeds than slow cars, so they can go farther in the same amount of time.

<u>Velocity</u> is speed in a certain direction. Two cars could be driving at the same speed but have different velocities if one of them goes north and the other goes south.

A car in motion rarely travels at the same exact speed the entire time. A car's speed and velocity often change. The car might speed up or slow down. This change in velocity is called <u>acceleration</u>. When the car picks up speed, it has positive acceleration. When the car loses speed, it has negative acceleration. People commonly refer to negative acceleration as <u>deceleration</u>. If you make the car go faster, you are accelerating the car. If the car starts moving slower, it is decelerating.

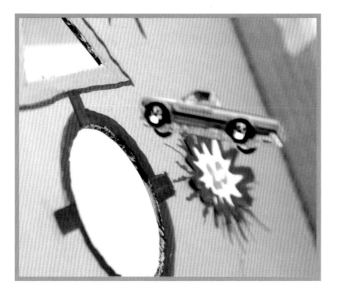

Quick Quiz

Tell whether each of the below scenarios is describing speed, velocity, or acceleration:

1. A TRAIN IS MOVING NORTH AT 120 MILES PER HOUR.

2. YOU RUN A MILE IN 7 MINUTES.

3. YOU HOP ON YOUR BIKE AND PEDAL REALLY HARD. AFTER 4 SECONDS OF PEDALING, YOU GO FROM TRAVELING 0 MILES PER HOUR TO 12 MILES PER HOUR.

Answers: 1) Velocity, 2) Speed, 3) Acceleration

FUN FACT

If you dropped a car straight down from a very high point, it would constantly accelerate, picking up speed, getting faster and faster until it reaches <u>terminal velocity</u>. Terminal velocity means the car is no longer accelerating. Its falling speed remains the same. This happens because of the force of air friction acting on the free-falling car. So what makes the car stop falling? Usually, when it hits the ground. The impact is a force that acts on the car, offsetting the force of gravity.

COLLISION COURSE

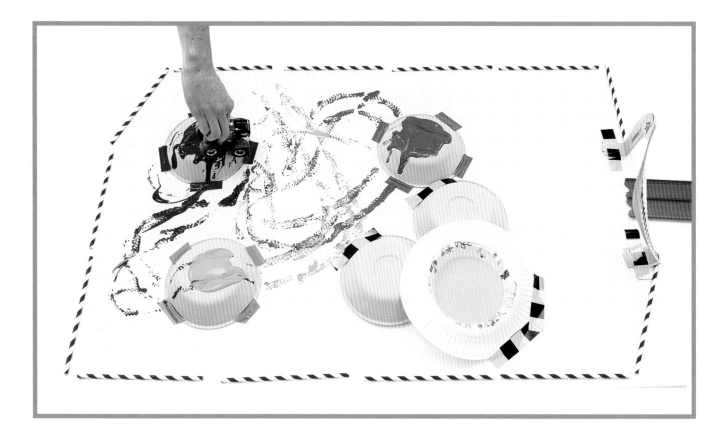

These awesome Hot Wheels hacks are super cool. You can race, twist, fly, and crash your cars. But guess what? That's exactly what car designers and engineers do in real life to make sure the cars they manufacture are safe and reliable.

Car designers *drive* the vehicles through obstacle courses, racing up and down ramps, around twisty turns, and across dangerous road surfaces just to make sure the cars handle safely. The cars are even put through collision testing by crashing them into solid barriers . . . *on purpose!* Sometimes, the crashed-up car ends up as a twisted, smashed mess, but this pile of metal provides car safety testers with lots of important information. Based on data collected before, during, and after the crash, they can study how the car measured up. They then use this information to improve the car's design to help it handle better on the road and make it even safer just in case of a collision.

Car manufacturers add lots of extra features to their cars to keep passengers safe. These include seat belts, airbags, and crumple zones. Always remember to wear your seat belt when riding in a car!

CRASH THIS

A car might look cool, but if people aren't safe traveling in it, then what's the point? Passenger comfort and safety are the most important parts of designing a car. Engineers use crash test dummies to understand what a passenger's experience will be in the car and predict injuries a person might sustain during a crash.

Crash test dummies might look like mannequins, but they're actually high-tech machines built to replicate the human body. They have spines, arms, and legs that very closely resemble the way a human is built. And since humans come in all shapes and sizes, crash test dummies also come in different weights, sizes, and genders! They even make dummies that resemble pet dogs!

IMAGINE THAT

Now that you know how car designers test cars they manufacture to make sure they are as safe and reliable as possible, you try it! Design an obstacle course that will measure the responsiveness, stability, and safety of your Hot Wheels cars. What changes would you make to the car to make it even better?

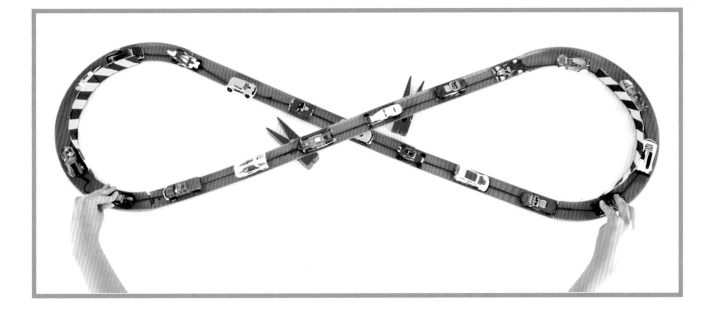

FUN FACT

Since cars drive all over the world in different conditions, it's important to test cars in extreme conditions . . . just in case. Cars are tested on icy roads, on dusty desert surfaces, in freezing temperatures, and in intense heat. How do you think a car would handle in extreme conditions? Imagine driving through a hot, wet rain forest. How would it be different from driving in the freezing Arctic?

INSIGHT
KIDS

PO Box 3088
San Rafael, CA 94912
www.insighteditions.com

Library of Congress Cataloging-in-Publication Data available.

ISBN: 978-1-64722-544-5

CEO: Raoul Goff
VP of Licensing and Partnerships: Vanessa Lopez
VP of Creative: Chrissy Kwasnik
VP of Manufacturing: Alix Nicholaeff
Associate Publisher: Sara Miller
Art Director: Stuart Smith
Designer: Brooke McCullum
Sponsoring Editor: Elizabeth Ovieda
Managing Editor: Vicki Jaeger
Production Editor: Jan Neal
Production Manager: Sam Taylor
Senior Production Manager, Subsidiary Rights: Lina s Palma

Additional art: P.47 VanderWolf Images/shutterstock.com

Insight Editions, in association with Roots of Peace, will plant two trees for each tree used in the manufacturing of this book. Roots of Peace is an internationally renowned humanitarian organization dedicated to eradicating land mines worldwide and converting war-torn lands into productive farms and wildlife habitats. Roots of Peace will plant two million fruit and nut trees in Afghanistan and provide farmers there with the skills and support necessary for sustainable land use.
Manufactured in China by Insight Editions

10 9 8 7 6 5 4 3 2 1